Praise for *Be a Change Champion* and Steven Gaffney's work

The following testimonials demonstrate how this book has made a difference in various industries and all levels of organizations.

"We have had the pleasure of working first hand with Steven and his team on a number of change initiatives over the past several years. His input and advice have contributed immensely to the success of those initiatives, particularly with respect to open and honest communication, a critical factor in any organization. This book, utilizing 10 straightforward Momentum Keys, a Change Completion Graph, and helpful real-life examples, provides an excellent roadmap for sustaining the momentum of successful change, whether it is organizational or personal. I highly recommend it."

-Jamie Sokalsky, CEO, Barrick Gold Corporation

"One of the greatest challenges a business leader has today is to help others understand and embrace the journey of change. In an ever-changing marketplace, competition comes from more directions. Customer demands shift more frequently. Time requirements are continually compressed, and new challenges emerge for the leadership team and the workforce – challenges to be more flexible, productive, efficient, creative, communicative, and team-oriented. Companies must adapt to survive under these new market conditions. The most successful companies, however, prosper in these times because their leadership focuses on energizing the entire organization towards a pursuit of a shared dream, and they find a way to maintain the organization's collective commitment to implementing the changes required to reach their goals. Steven Gaffney is an industry leader in helping both individuals and organizations deal with change. In *Be a Change Champion*, Steven has found a way to break down the complex nature of mastering momentum during change initiatives. His 10 keys to success offer an insightful roadmap that can help leaders truly understand the impediments to successful change. In addition, the book provides readers valuable tools and methods to break through the barriers that slow down the momentum a changing organization needs to achieve its goals."

-Stu Shea, Business Leader and Intelligence Professional, former President and Chief Operating Officer, Leidos

"Be a Change Champion" is an insightful, quick, and meaningful read for anyone who leads a business. It's a book that all stakeholders can, and should, read time and time again. If you are facing any obstacle in implementing a new strategy, you will be able to directly apply Steve's simple, yet effective, stages in running a clean, motivated, and honest organization. As Steve presents in the book, reinforcement, repetition, and proactive honesty do not end at the beginning of change, but run continuously throughout successful ventures."

-JD Kathuria, Founder & CEO, WashingtonExec

"Steven has done it again. This work should be of monumental consequence to all who need to effect and manage change for success. Change is essential in business. Continued success demands it. But anyone contemplating change should read this book carefully. Take Steven's core point to heart.... change is not a one-time event. Rather, it is a process that will challenge the most wise and most dedicated change agent. Be prepared for a grind. Use the advice contained in this work. Think about the examples. Put his graphic on your wall and review it daily. Be glad Steven has produced this work for you."

-Larry Cox, COO, EMM Technology

"Having led the transformation of a 45-year-old company to two new companies with distinct strategic intents, I agree with the challenge of maintaining enterprise momentum. Steven's new book identifies the most common challenges to sustaining the momentum that is required to successfully implement a major change program. He also offers practical solutions to these challenges, many of which I utilized with great success."

-Doug Wagoner, President, Services & Solutions Sector, SAIC

"Steven has hit another home run. Change can be debilitating, even to a good organization and management team. Steven's insights to keep positive change moving forward are clear and concise…a must-read for change leaders."

-Steve Schaefer, Aerospace and Defense Consultant and former Vice President, COBHAM

"Steven's book is a must-read for anyone contemplating a period of substantive organizational change. I work with companies struggling with ways to strengthen their corporate ethical cultures, and Steven's practical steps for organizing, executing, and maintaining change momentum are bound to be a game-changer for organizations striving to improve their ethical performance."

-Eric R. Feldman, Managing Director, Corporate Ethics and Compliance Programs, Affiliated Monitors, Inc. and Former Inspector General, U.S. National Reconnaissance Office

"Steven's new book, *Be a Change Champion*, hit me at an opportune time. We recently implemented several key changes in our organizational structure and I had been looking for ways to avoid loss of focus and momentum. The book offers a number of great ideas and provides thought-provoking concepts to keep morale high and maintain energy as we move forward. He packs a tremendous amount of beneficial and helpful material in just a few, easy-to-implement pages."

-Ken Smith, Executive Director, Alabama League of Municipalities

"Gaffney has cracked the code on corporate reorganizations by serving up a series of accessible, pragmatic tools that empower people over process."

**-Derek Edgar, Director of Marketing, DePuy Synthes,
a Johnson & Johnson Company**

"This book brings together two critical factors for the success of any leader – the ability to lead and sustain change, plus Steven Gaffney's acclaimed thinking on the subject. Change is never easy, however, it is the hallmark of a true leader, and Steven guides us through everything we need to know about leading and sustaining change in this new book. Initiating change is difficult, sustaining change is even more difficult, and bringing change to completion is most difficult of all. Steven's 10 Momentum Keys are exactly what we need to guide us through the process."

**-L. William Varner, President, Mission, Cyber & Intelligence Group,
ManTech International Corporation**

"Steven Gaffney brings to the written word the same engaging, captivating and thought provoking style that makes him such an effective speaker. *Be a Change Champion* is a pragmatic guide for dealing with the only constant in the world…change. The examples he uses will resonate with the reader and the advice he offers is sound. I recommend this book for anyone who aspires to be an impactful change champion."

-Charles Wright, President, Public Sector Services, Travelers

"Throughout my career I have led significant change initiatives both in the private and public environments, and have been faced with many of the factors discussed in *Be a Change Champion.* Steven's insights into these momentum factors are absolutely on the mark. The issues he discusses occur in both small and large projects and being able to effectively manage these factors are critical for success."

**-Jack Pellegrino, Director, Department of
Purchasing and Contracting, County of San Diego**

"Most people profess to support change. The problem, however, is that people fail to realize how they personally may be stalling or blocking a change initiative, and they ultimately blame everyone else when the change fails. Steven's book bridges that gap, brings clarity to all participants involved in a change, and creates a logical path forward so any organizational change will be a success."

-Tom Kritzell, President, Smiths Power

"I have worked with Steven for over seven years to help fix some of the change-related issues of major projects that our internal change management processes have been unable to address. During my last project, I was plagued with every issue that Steve talks about in his book, and I believe that this is a 'must-read' and a perfect 'checklist' for every manager about to embark on a major strategic initiative for an organization. Steven's methods have proven successful each time I have incorporated them into my projects. This book is long overdue!"

-Klaus Heerwig, Senior Associate, Booz Allen Hamilton

"45+ years in government and private industry have allowed me to experience the infinite ways people address change. Today's executives would do well to prepare themselves, and their organizations, with the tools to implement and sustain the change actions needed to reach their desired change objectives. Gaffney's insights and track record of guiding organizations through this minefield provide a confidence-building framework for any enterprise seeking a better way to achieve success."

-Bill Schmieder, President, Raytheon International, Europe

"Steve Gaffney's insights continue to amaze me. In the world that we live in, where change is the only constant, it's our ability to plan for it, adapt to it, and learn from it that will separate organizations. Steve's approach is a well-thought-out strategy that is a must read for everybody."

-Scott DiGiammarino, CEO and Founder, Reel Potential and former Executive at American Express Financial Advisors

"Regardless of industry, all leaders can benefit from reading this book. While going through his Momentum Keys, I kept having 'ah-ha!' moments as to why I have witnessed so many organizational changes fail. Steven provides practical and applicable tools to maintain momentum during a change, as well as clear examples to demonstrate his points. I highly recommend this book and can confidently say it has improved the way I will manage change moving forward."

-Max Schindler, TV Director/Producer and Media Consultant,
Broadcast Management Group

"Too many times, we see common organizational themes of having '*too many chefs in the kitchen*,' not letting '*perfect be the enemy of good enough*,' or '*diplomacy vs. naysayers*' just to name just a few. Seeing Steven Gaffney put structure and substance into addressing these organizational challenges was quite refreshing and necessary. The material in *Be a Change Champion* provides an easy-to-implement approach for tackling the acute challenges of effectuating change in an organization in an efficient and positive manner. This book is a great resource for anyone who either leads or participates in change in his or her organization."

-Zachary Gifford, Associate Director, Systemwide Risk Management,
the California State University

"Once again, Steven gives us practical tools to use on a common and important challenge that faces all organizations. Leading change is the challenge of our time, as the pace and imperative of change makes this a critical skill for effective leaders in every enterprise."

-Jeff MacLauchlan, Vice President, Corporate Development,
Lockheed Martin Corporation

"Steven Gaffney has worked with me both as a consultant and a mentor. The insights provided in his new book are as relevant, insightful, and useful as those he provided me when I was tackling the challenges of managing change in a multi-billion dollar organization. Steven's pragmatic recommendations on maintaining the momentum required to successfully implement change, as well as the proactive steps one can take to combat organizational inertia ensure that I will always keep the book close at hand. This book provides a framework for implementing change, and in today's world, there is no skill more valuable in business."

-Gene Colabatistto, President, Defense and Security, CAE

"I had the opportunity and privilege to work with Steven Gaffney in advising and supporting us in improving the engagement levels of our employees at Barrick Gold Corporation during a very difficult time for our industry and company, characterized by high levels of uncertainty and unexpected changes in the global context.

Steven played an outstanding role by influencing and coaching our leaders to maintain momentum, continue delivering better than expected results, and preserve the morale and motivation of our employees even when difficult and unpopular decisions have been made and implemented. His unique ability to make the complex and unattainable task of managing people´s expectations and willingness to deliver easier and possible is one of his competitive advantages.

In this new book, Steven provides an excellent and easy-to-implement toolkit of applicable concepts that makes it easier for leaders and anyone responsible for results to deal with exponential change which could be cumbersome to manage."

-David Riano, HR Business Partner-Northern Latin America, SAP

"It is rare to be provided with a set of tools that facilitate open and honest communication, and in so doing, help you get the job done more effectively and expeditiously. Steven Gaffney provides just such a tool set-a powerful arsenal, really- that helps leaders, teams, and workforces blast through barriers to effective communication. The result is an approach to workforce communication that is less polluted with innuendo and supposition; thereby, allowing frank, but non-personal, dialogue about issues facing an organization. This is material you can put into practice immediately for tangible results!"

-Marion Eggenberger,
Department of Navy Customer Support Director

"Steve Gaffney brings such a fresh perspective to how to run your business, how to be an effective leader, and how to manage change. In my time working with him, it is apparent that he truly is a change champion. If he was being completely 'honest,' Steve would list himself as one of the top 10 factors to sustaining momentum during a period of change."

-Gary Rosen, Senior Vice President for Operations, Leidos

"Steven Gaffney's *Be a Change Champion* is a must-do; not just a must-read. The principles and practices he presents add up to extremely useful strategies in keeping the momentum going toward a planned change. Most of us have great ideas and plans that get cut short or cut off by ourselves or our (company) people. Don't let that happen, follow *Be a Change Champion* for a change!"

-Neal Arita, Executive Director,
Sheet Metal Contractors Association

"Once again in his newest book, Steven Gaffney's straightforward and easy to understand messaging allows anyone - from top tier executives to those just starting their upward rise - to be successful and powerful. *Be a Change Champion* is a must-read for everyone. For the largest and smallest businesses, Gaffney's message is clear: to be a change champion, use his 10 "Momentum Keys" and open the path to greater success!"

-Avery Mann, former Head of Communications and
Marketing for Fox TV's *America's Most Wanted*

"The vast majority of change initiatives either fail or don't deliver the desired results. Steven has successfully tackled the difficult subject of change management by breaking the problem into 10 factors that will sustain momentum and avoid failure. Change management is one of the greatest challenges in business, and Steven has provided an excellent toolbox that will push your next change initiative to success!"

-Chet Claudon, President and General Manager,
COBHAM Tactical Communications & Surveillance

"I recently reached out to Steven for advice related to an organizational change issue because I didn't want my company to fall into the age-old traps related to change. One of the many things I've learned from him is that change is constant and must be dealt with timely and effectively to ensure future success. Not only do his strategies from *Be a Change Champion* work for keeping momentum going, but his energy and passion are inspiring and bleed into everyone around him. I know the book will be extremely helpful to anyone involved in a major organizational change, myself included."

-Debbie Thurman, Vice President of Contracts and Procurement, URS

"Every organization faces change. Steven provides leaders the tools and resources they need to guide their teams through change – to help them manage the human aspect of change."

-Cheryl Seminara, Director, Employee Development Division, FEMA

"Steven delivered amazing results for our company that far exceeded our expectations. He is a dynamic speaker who is entertaining, impactful, and provides meaningful and results-oriented material that we continue to use every day. Steven opened our eyes on honest communication, and as a result, has helped us to articulate and solidify our corporate culture."

-Greg and Lynn Kiyan, Owners, Air Central Inc.

"Steven Gaffney is the first to create an insightful roadmap on how to successfully navigate through the change process and keep momentum going in an organization. *Be a Change Champion* is a profound and useful book on making and sustaining change in order to propel your organization into the future."

-Tina Kuhn, Senior Vice President, Sotera Defense Solutions, Inc

"Steven Gaffney has written an excellent book for any company going through organizational change. Steven's 10 Momentum Keys are an easy-to-follow roadmap to greatly improve any organizational change initiative."

-Paul Falker, Corporate Vice President for National Intelligence, Vistronix

"Organizational change is critical to success in business, yet is one of the most complex problems I have ever faced. Steven delivers straightforward tools that any leader will benefit from reading in a format that can be used immediately to improve an organization's success with change. *Be a Change Champion* brings a fresh perspective to how teams can break down the barriers to change."

-Peder Jungck, Vice President and Chief Technology Officer, Intelligence & Security, BAE Systems

"Steven Gaffney's newest book on America's 'change fatigue' in organizations will make your company dramatically more effective. The book inspires you with new processes to create and establish agile patterns for team decisions, as well as robust new ideas for execution and best possible results for shareholder growth."

-Dave Lahey, President & CEO, Predictive Success Corporation

"Steven's lectures, workshops, and books have changed the way we think, operate and most importantly, the way we treat each other. Steven has positively changed our culture."

-Brigadier General Frank Kelley, Former Commander, Marine Corps Systems Command

"Steven has captured the essence of how to ensure change initiatives will succeed. Building on the foundations established in *Just Be Honest*, the tools Steven provides are practical, effective, and can be easily implemented by anyone responsible for executing change initiatives."

-Chris Reil, Vice President, Sensor Electronics, COBHAM

"Before I read *Be a Change Champion*, I will admit that I didn't see the hardcore business case for what Steven Gaffney did for companies and how different he was from other consulting firms. After reading this book, however, I realized why he gets the results that he does. I had to sit back and really think about how profound his strategies and tactics were for my business and my clients. Any team that has ever decided to do something significant, something great, has to first figure out what Steven has already mastered. This book will flatten any team's learning curve on how to gain and maintain momentum. It breaks down the keys to why momentum is fleeting and how to avoid the loss. It shows you how the energy of change is maintained and how to get things done with velocity. This book is packed with strategies you can use to break down the barriers to cooperation that plague most companies. If you don't have Steven's principles as your organizational priority, your only option is to put your head down and power through the pain. But, you can put this no-frills powerful book to work for you immediately. He shows you how to free yourself and your team from those long-standing limiting beliefs and habits. If you have a team that builds mental roadblocks to getting things done or loses momentum before you reach your goals, this book is for you. It won't take you long to see what I saw. Dysfunction does have a cure... Thank you, Steven."

-Zemira Z. Jones, Management Consultant and former President of ABC Radio

"Steven Gaffney has a unique talent in being able to tie some of his easy-to-implement, foundational premises into the solution to a more challenging problem. In *Be a Change Champion*, he blends his legendary honest and direct communication techniques with new material on mastering change and momentum. This book excels because it is written using real-life examples. His advice is not merely conjecture, but based on real world situations that have impacted many leaders out there. Keep this book as a reference as you embark upon change in your organization, and I suspect that you will be pleasantly surprised at the outcomes."

-Paul Gentile, Senior Vice President and Cyber Solutions General Manager, ManTech International Corporation

BE A CHANGE CHAMPION

MASTERING MOMENTUM

10 Factors for Sustaining the Boom and Avoiding the Bust of Change

ALSO BY STEVEN GAFFNEY

*Just Be Honest: Authentic Communication
Strategies That Get Results and Last a Lifetime*

*Honesty Works! Real-World Solutions to Common
Problems at Work and Home*

*Honesty Sells: How to Make More Money and
Increase Business Profits* (with Colleen Francis)

*Guide to Increasing Communication Flow Up,
Down, and Across Your Organization*

21 Rules for Delivering Difficult Messages

BE A CHANGE
CHAMPION
MASTERING MOMENTUM
10 Factors for Sustaining the Boom and Avoiding the Bust of Change

BY STEVEN GAFFNEY

JMG PUBLISHING

Be a Change Champion. Mastering Momentum: 10 Factors for Sustaining the Boom and Avoiding the Bust of Change
by Steven Gaffney

ISBN- 978-0-9897159-9-7

Published by JMG Publishing
Fairfax, VA

For general information on Steven Gaffney's products in the U.S., please call (703) 241-7796 or email us at info@stevengaffney.com. Visit www.stevengaffney.com.

This book is dedicated to all the people who have the courage, tenacity, and commitment to make the changes they would like to see in the world. In particular, to my Mom and Dad, who have shown me that you can make anything happen that you are willing to MAKE happen. Thank you for making me into the man I am today and who I will hopefully become. You have shown me that anything I can dream is possible.

Acknowledgements

There were many people involved in the production of this book. I would first like to acknowledge my clients, participants, family, and friends whose encouragement, contributions, and wisdom helped bring this book to life.

To the staff of Steven Gaffney Company, in particular Breyana Lehman, who spearheaded this project and ultimately made it happen.

Special thanks to those who helped edit, add to, review, and advise on the draft of this book: Nina Taylor, John Gaffney, Larry Cox, Lisa Gaffney, Alan Weiss, and John Peragine.

Thank you to everyone who provided us a testimonial for the book. I'm so thankful that its content and the work we have done together have made such an impact. As I have often said, together we can make a difference.

In addition, I wanted to thank Stu Shea, who first raised the issues of sustaining momentum during change initiatives and started me down the journey that resulted in the completion of this book.

A special acknowledgement to Tu-Anh, who has always been and will always remain the angel in my life and my eternal beacon of hope.

Introduction–Sick of Change?

It would not surprise me if those of you who are reading this book are sick of change. When you really think about it, why wouldn't you be? The truth is that 70% of organizational or cultural changes fail to achieve their intended objectives. This fact alone has turned most people into skeptics who simply do not believe change can succeed and grow tired from even thinking about it!

Being an expert on honest communication and knowing that the big problem in organizations is not what people say to each other but what they do not say, I have come to realize that there is a critical missing component when it comes to change. That missing component is everything that remains unsaid—the unspoken ideas and issues. You can't fix a problem unless you know about it, and you can't use an idea to improve the change unless someone tells you the idea. The unsaid has a significant impact on the pace and success of change! Because of our expertise in "getting the unsaid said," we naturally started being brought into organizations that were launching and executing major change initiatives.

After experiencing success using our communication content, our clients began to ask us to develop core strategies to help keep up the momentum, motivation, and morale related to change initiatives—so we did. In the course of teaching these strategies, we realized there are no books out there dedicated to keeping up the momentum of a change, hence the genesis of Be a Change Champion.

Over time, our work on boosting and maintaining momentum has expanded to become a significant part of our business, including how to lead through times of uncertainty, how to influence with or without authority, and our legendary process on how to turn any organizational idea into a plan with accountability in 2 hours and 18 minutes. We have been involved in everything from a Fortune 500 company splitting into two new, entirely separate companies to helping a company through a massive reorientation from a customer-facing segment to a market-facing segment. We have also been brought in on changes to turn a traditional command-and-control business model to a matrix organization, and we've been able to assist in a major product launch that involved a change in the way an industry will forever handle its services.

Whether you're leading, participating in, or observing a change, big or small, in this book you will find specific strategies, techniques, and tools to boost motivation and momentum and ultimately achieve success. (Keep in mind that all of these strategies, techniques, and tools can also be used in your personal life at home as well.) I hope you enjoy the book, and please let me know your feedback as well as your success stories!

Visit our website, www.stevengaffney.com, for many free resources, including videos, articles, and podcasts on aspects of communication, leadership, and change that you can use at work and home.

The Foundation Gap

Change often starts with a bang, but it's usually only a matter of time before it drifts off course or grinds to a screeching halt. Research cited in Harvard Business Review makes the situation sound hopeless: 70 percent of organizational and cultural changes fail to achieve their desired outcomes. Why does this happen?

For almost two decades, I have worked with clients on numerous change initiatives, both small and large, including mergers, acquisitions, and reorganizations. Interestingly enough, KPMG International found that 83 percent of acquisitions and mergers fail to achieve their intended value. Through my work with clients, I've come to realize that these changes usually fail due to the execution rather than design of the change. There is simply a foundational gap in resources and knowledge about how to generate and maintain the motivation, momentum, and morale surrounding the initiative. Essentially, the change dies from lack of energy; it runs out of gas.

When it comes to change, there are numerous books and other materials out there. There are books on managing change, dealing with change, organizational changes, and so forth, but there is little about how to maintain momentum once a change is launched. This is the only book that we know of that is dedicated to keeping up the momentum of a change.

I've been fortunate enough to work with some of the top executives of some of the best companies in the world, and I have learned greatly from them as well as from what we have been able to contribute. As a result, I've discovered there are 10 critical factors to mastering momentum and avoiding the bust of change. Whether you are launching a major company strategy, a team project, or even a change within yourself, the following 10 Momentum Keys and the accompanying Change Completion Graph can help your change go from bust to boom. If you are the official leader of the change, a participant in it, or even an observer, this book can help you make a critical difference to the initiative so you can be a change champion.

As you begin learning about the keys (and later when you refer back to them), be sure to consult the Change Completion Graph on pages 36-37. This graph demonstrates that there are always obstacles at work to undermine motivation and momentum. The arrows pointing downward reveal those momentum killers such as unnecessary complications, resistance, the endless search for new and better ideas, scope creep, perfectionism, and low morale. The arrows pointing upward display the attitudes and actions that counteract those killers and boost momentum. Using the following 10 keys in conjunction with understanding the graph will help you boost motivation, keep change on track, and ultimately achieve success.

MOMENTUM KEY 1:
Beware of Exit Ramps

L et's face it. Many change initiatives just don't go well. I have partnered with many teams who are working through a change initiative and experiencing numerous problems. In these situations, I always ask the group, "What is the overall endgame of the change? What will success look like?" Every time I pose these questions, participants are unable to provide a crystal clear answer or if they do, the answers are not consistent across the group.

After all, the desired outcome of an organizational change must be clear to everyone on your team. If it is not clear in peoples' minds, they cannot possibly clearly explain it to others, let alone keep up the momentum. Understanding the ultimate outcome will keep you on the road to your destination and prevent you from taking an exit ramp prematurely and missing your goal altogether.

Don't Circle Back

Many exit ramps can tempt people to take detours along the way to their destination. As the graph shows, some people might be tempted to revisit the approved plan and some might even be tempted to revisit the original ideas.

Don't let this happen; these are momentum killers. Many organizations allow re-litigating and revisiting of decisions, but I have only seen this result in wasted time, resources, and money as well as lost motivation among employees. The revisiting of decisions also disempowers the leaders involved. The best organizations make decisions and move forward. This is critical in gaining and maintaining momentum.

Of course, there are times to reopen a decision, but they are rare; ideally, there should be certain criteria that must be met in order to reopen a decision. Before you launch an initiative, create the standards about what needs to happen before a decision can be reopened. A good example would be anything that would make achieving the outcome impossible — such as a major disruption in time or a dramatic change in projected costs. Even these types of issues can be a slippery slope, and this is an issue that should be given special attention and treatment.

I'm sure you have heard of "change fatigue" in organizations, but I have found that it's not always change fatigue at work, but indecision fatigue! Establish a pattern with your team that once a decision is made, you move forward and spend 100 percent of your energy in executing the decision for the best possible results.

To keep the team on the right road, one tactical idea is to use various ways to remind the team of the outcome you are trying to accomplish and how success will look when it's completed. Then, reinforce and repeat. For example, post a reminder sign of the goal by each person's desk. These reminders will help people choose the right priorities in their daily work and prevent the change initiative from becoming another case of out of sight, out of mind.

MOMENTUM KEY 2:
Expect Problems

As the saying goes in the military, "No plan of battle ever survives contact with the enemy." This saying doesn't mean we shouldn't plan; it just means we should do so with the understanding that the original plan is going to need modifications along the way. Such adjustments are nearly unavoidable because once you launch your plan, you are going to learn things you could never have anticipated when you first created it.

Expectations are critical here. Often, people forget that even the best, most well-thought-out plans will still need to be adjusted or modified. Instead, they create a perception that once a certain stage is completed, the team is "in the clear." Change doesn't work this way, and it is likely that you will experience many additional complications or issues, some that will even affect deadlines and budget. This is why expectations must be managed.

You can manage these expectations by letting people know from the beginning that there will be problems and issues along the way, but no matter what, success will be achieved in the end. Otherwise, when people encounter a bump in the road, they immediately think, "See, I knew this would happen," and they begin to fight the change because they don't believe it can succeed. That is when all the naysayers waiting in the wings come out and make things worse. (We will talk more about naysayers and how to manage them in Key 7.)

One of the best examples of this scenario is found in IT. When new IT initiatives are launched, no matter how well a program is designed, there are always bugs and challenges. If the expectations aren't properly managed, people blame the initiative and think the new program is a failure. However, if they know there will be kinks to work out, then they can contribute valuable feedback rather than complaints and patiently wait for a positive result. What makes the difference is whether expectations are managed.

Use Measurement to Your Advantage
Establishing an expectation that progress will be measured and reported is also helpful here. This lets people know that there will be objective measurements, and adjustments will be made as needed. One of my clients was working on a spacecraft program and, during the design phase, they

had a problem with the weight of the payload. The project manager put up a sign on the doorway where every team member entered that displayed the current design weight of the payload versus the maximum allowed weight. Every day each employee saw the challenge. Each day everyone saw what had to be achieved and was able to identify the gap between the goal and reality. Adjustments were made, and, eventually, the team made the weight.

A good practice when implementing any change is to build in a mechanism to help mitigate the challenges that will ultimately come up. For example, as part of the IT initiative, the team can set up a central FAQ page as well as an inbox or forum for people to submit their feedback, concerns, and unanswered questions. Implementing this helps people to feel heard, share solutions, and feel more confident in the change moving forward.

I have found that leaders who communicate this idea of expecting problems and manage expectations accordingly have a workforce that maintains momentum and who are not rattled when problems crop up. When employees know from the beginning that the expectation is to plan, execute, and adjust along the way, they have a better ability to weather difficulty and stay on track.

One practical idea to help encourage this mindset is to keep your written plans updated, current, and readily accessible to the entire team (see upward arrow 3 on the graph on page 36). Doing so helps employees not to be sidetracked by potential options and ideas. If delays occur and adjustments are needed, adjust the timelines and notify the affected parties as necessary. Meeting deadlines and hitting goals is satisfying; keeping plans and deadlines up to date is a great way to keep motivation intact and maintain momentum.

MOMENTUM KEY 3:
"Why" Matters

People are often so focused on the execution of change that they lose sight of the benefit and value that will come when the change is complete. Sometimes, people even become so focused on the difficulty of achieving the change that it leads to resistance (see downward arrow 2 on the graph on page 36). When people feel this way, it can result in a negative cycle of increasing difficulty and resistance about moving forward. Focusing on the benefits and value of the desired end game of the change (see upward arrow 2) increases the likelihood of achieving the goal and ultimately reaping those benefits.

Therefore, one of the most important things to share at the very beginning of the process is why the change is happening. In fact, in terms of momentum, knowing why a change is happening (and continuing to remind people of the why) is often more important than knowing all the details of executing it. Furthermore, as one of my clients pointed out, when you tell people why the change is happening, they will often help you figure out the how. As they do that, they become more engaged in the change process.

Recently, one of my clients was in charge of executing a change in his organization, and he spent the majority of his time explaining to his group why the change was happening and little time on what the change even was. His two peers, who were also launching the same change in their respective groups, focused on what was happening: who was reporting to whom, filling in the boxes, and so forth. The result was that my client's group immediately moved out on the change; the employees were enthusiastic, and the change was accomplished. In the other two groups, employees resisted, dragged out the process of executing the change, and, ultimately, the change was never fully implemented.

As a side note, one of the number one ways to help employees improve job performance is to explain why something needs to be done. This is even more important than detailing what needs to be done. The lesson is that when people know the why, they can often fill in the gray areas that are inevitable with any performance change or challenge.

What's in It for Me?

Keep in mind that when you're explaining why a change needs to happen, the most powerful explanation incorporates what is in it for the receiver of the message. How will a change initiative benefit your employees? This can be tricky because organizations tend to focus on the change's benefit to the organization itself. Saying that an initiative is good for the overall company is nice, helpful, and important to building a solid company culture. However, with the amount of layoffs that have happened in organizational changes lately in response to economic pressures, many employees need more. They tend to think, "How does this change relate to and affect me personally?"

They need why messages that acknowledge the personal benefits of the initiative. For example, a why message that says, "This will help the company increase revenue and be more profitable," probably will not move the needle in improving employee motivation and implementation. However, a message that might work would be, "This change will help the company increase revenue and profits, resulting in a stronger company that will allow us to thrive in the future and take advantage of opportunities, so there will be opportunities for you as we grow." This type of message tends to capture people's attention. If you would like more on this, ask for our upcoming booklet on the 6 Core Drivers of Human Behavior — "SIRGES."

MOMENTUM KEY 4:
Use Resistance-Busting Questions

B reaking through resistance is critical to the launch of any change initiative. One way to do this is to use one or a combination of the following three questions. I call them the Resistance-Busting Questions (see upward arrow 2 on the graph on page 36). You do not need to use all of these questions for a breakthrough.

Knowing which questions you use and how you use them will have a lot to do with who is being resistant. Depending on the politics, roles of the people involved, and sensitivity of the situation, these questions can be asked privately or publicly with your team. Sometimes, it can be helpful to meet with someone you know is resistant before a meeting and ask the questions before you bring them up in front of the rest of the group. Remember that resistance is not necessarily bad. Someone may be seeing something that you are missing. Also, hidden resistance is worse than vocal resistance. It is better for people to resist vocally and publicly rather than outside the group or in the hallways. These questions are effective tools for moving the conversation toward finding solutions and maintaining momentum.

QUESTION 1: "WHAT WOULD YOU SUGGEST?"

Anyone can pick ideas and plans apart — that's easy. The hard part is providing ideas and suggestions for improvement. I have seen many changes stalled because a lone naysayer is holding everyone else hostage. The solution is to ask the naysayer for a better suggestion. If the naysayer doesn't have one, then take a stand and let that person know that the change will be moving forward, but their ideas are welcome in the future. (Obviously, you need to be cautious about using this question and the response; it depends who you are talking to.)

QUESTION 2: "WHAT WOULD IT TAKE FOR YOU TO AGREE?"

This is a great question to use — especially when the resistant person is critical for buy-in. This is also a great question because it can reveal whether the current plan is just missing certain pieces or whether the plan itself is half-baked. Do not be afraid to ask this question and pursue the answers, and in doing so, you can unlock the resistance, move forward with velocity, and set the stage for great change momentum.

CHAPTER 4

Variations of this question can be used in all types of situations. For example, if someone can't support an element related to what you're working on, you can ask, "What would it take for you to consider it?" or "What would it take for you to be more open to my suggestion?" These questions allow you to maintain your stance and can reveal that the two parties may be closer than they think. For example, I have seen people resist an idea because of the timeline or how the idea is implemented; they are not actually resistant to the overall idea itself. Asking this type of question allows the dialog to continue and can uncover the specific areas of resistance. One golden tip that I have coached many people to use when they are probing with someone is to assume there is more to the story.

Gathering support for an idea can be a little like trying to open a safe. You may have four out of five digits correct, but if you don't have the fifth, the safe won't open. A question of this nature helps you to discover what the final digit is so that you can crack the code.

QUESTION 3: "CAN YOU LIVE WITH IT?"

This question is often used as a last resort, but it can reveal how large the issue actually is for that person. It is also the right question to ask when you are at an impasse. The answer reveals whether this is a non-negotiable for the person or simply a want or desire. When people are asked this question, they will often see that the issue they are hung up on is not critical — especially if they are reminded of the end game and encouraged to focus on the big picture.

I've seen many organizations waste a tremendous amount of time discussing, revisiting, and arguing over something that is not ultimately a deal breaker. I was working with an organization that wanted to get every team member's buy-in for an initiative. The person advocating the change had everyone's buy-in except for one person. Taking my coaching, he asked the one holdout, "What would you suggest?" She responded, "I don't know." He then asked, "What would it take for you to agree?" She responded, "I'm not sure, I need to think about it." Finally, he used the final question: "If you're not sure of a suggestion or what it would take for you to agree, can you live with it?" She thought for a moment, said "Yes," and then moved forward and advocated for the change.

Later on, I circled back with her and asked her for her thought process. She shared, "I couldn't think of a suggestion and I wasn't quite clear for myself what it would take to support it. However, when I was asked if I could live with it, I realized I was holding up an initiative all because it had to be 'my way or the highway,' and I realized the silliness of my resistance. It wasn't that big of a deal. So that question helped me get clear on what was really important and that I should not be holding up the process."

MOMENTUM KEY 5:
Build on the Three Core Non-Negotiables

I have found three non-negotiables that are critical for executing change. All three increase communication flow. When we negotiate these non-negotiables, the pace of change will slow dramatically, making the change more costly and jeopardizing its full implementation. Using the non-negotiables to your advantage will boost momentum and motivation.

NON-NEGOTIABLE 1: MAKE AND KEEP COMMITMENTS WITHOUT HAVING TO CHECK IN.

When an organization's culture values making and keeping commitments, there is no reason for you to have to go out of your way to check in with people. Think about how

Change

HIGH

Motivation and Focus

ARROW 1:
Complicating things

ARROW 2:
Resistance (i.e. Plan/idea is not good)

ARROW 3:
Uncover additional steps and potential options/ideas

- Remember, make progress, not perfection
- Hold the line of the original scope and end state

- Confront/address objection. Don't let resistance take a foothold
- Ask the 3 Resistance Busting Questions
- Focus on the value and benefits of the outcome
- Get key influencers' buy in

- Evaluate through the original scope and end state
- Update the plan so it is always current
- Keep moving forward and simplify where you can

FOCUS AND DETERM

LOW

START

Timeframe

Completion Graph

ARROW 4:

Scope creep (A slippery slope that ruins motivation and slows down progress)

- Remind people of the original scope and end state
- Take items outside the scope and save them to be done later
- Keep moving forward to make progress, not perfection

ARROW 5:

Temptation to revisit and take more time to make the plan better. It is not perfect.

- The plan is good enough to move forward
- Each day we delay, no one gets the benefit of the project
- Hold the line and finish; we can always adjust and/or take on additional aspects later

ARROW 6:

Morale is "doom and gloom"

- Achieve quick wins and celebrate along the way
- If we focus on successes, we get more successes

NATION OF THE TEAM

of Completion   FINISH

many policies and procedures exist to simply ensure that people are doing what they said they would do. This creates bureaucracy, red tape, and redundant procedures due to lack of trust—people don't believe that other people are actually going to do what they are supposed to do. This belief slows down an organization and eats away its profitability.

It can be so difficult to find time to implement change; spending time and energy checking in can be demotivating to you and your team, and it can short-circuit momentum. People hate to be micromanaged. By choosing to trust each person to manage their own work as well as their part in the change initiative, you build trust and embolden them to take proactive and courageous action. All of this helps propel momentum throughout the change process.

If you find yourself checking up with people, it is probably because of lack of trust. Have a meeting where you are upfront and resolve these trust issues rather than developing a culture of babysitting and policing.

NON-NEGOTIABLE 2: PROACTIVE HONESTY.

A culture of proactive honesty means that we are upfront about our problems, challenges, and issues. This includes notifying the appropriate parties if you can't do what you said you'd do according to the established deadline. For example, if something is due by Friday at 5:00 and you know on Tuesday that you are unlikely to get that finished, it's time to notify anyone who would want to know. Let those people know a new timeline that will work and anything that is needed to get the job done. It is also a chance to communicate any suggestions that can help moving forward.

I call this proactive honesty because often people say, "Well, no one asked me." Establishing a non-negotiable about proactive honesty sets the expectation that waiting to be asked is not an appropriate excuse. Sharing problems, issues, ideas, and suggestions should be an expectation for the performance of any job, and this non-negotiable reflects that. After all, discovering on the deadline day (or after!) that a deliverable is not completed is extremely demotivating, and will plant seeds of distrust and result in people creating policies and procedures to compensate. Upward arrow 3 on the Change Completion graph is a good reminder that keeping plans updated and current – by using proactive honesty – helps to keep the team focused and motivated.

NON-NEGOTIABLE 3: STRAIGHT-LINE COMMUNICATION.

This simply means that if you have a problem with someone, you go directly to the person and speak with him or her rather than talking to others about that person or an issue. Direct communication also means that if you need something from someone, you should go directly to that person and not rely on the grapevine to do the communicating for you. This sounds easy, yet people often do not do it because it requires an open, honest dialogue that can be uncomfortable.

Here is the challenge: When organizational changes are underway, people tend to get upset and have issues with each other. They end up going to other people, spreading rumors and misinformation (this often happens by accident and isn't intended to be malicious), which produces unnecessary drama and disconnection and ultimately undermines morale. Pretty soon, a simple problem becomes a complex issue that sucks in others' energy and wastes tremendous time with extra meetings and so forth.

If you can learn to avoid these issues by communicating directly, you will help your change initiatives succeed because you won't have relationship issues weighing you down and distracting you from the destination. I'm not advocating that everyone in the organization needs to go directly to the CEO or the key leader to discuss issues; obviously this is about being sensitive and respecting reporting lines, but I do know that we need to remind ourselves to communicate directly so that we don't slip into the default mode of avoiding confrontation with the appropriate person.

Another important part of direct communication is refusing to engage and perpetuate grapevine information. When we were children, we realized that when somebody tells somebody who tells somebody, the information becomes distorted. Unfortunately, adults in the workplace hear grapevine information (or as I like to call it, the corporate telephone game), and they think and act as if it is the truth. For all of these reasons, direct communication is desirable whenever possible. Remember, the shortest, most efficient path between two points is a straight line.

The issues addressed in these three non-negotiables (doing what you're supposed to do, proactive honesty, and direct communication) enable organizations to function effectively. I recommend having a candid discussion as part of your next team meeting where you establish these non-negotiables and start to put them into practice. Instituting these non-negotiables in your organization's culture can prevent small issues from becoming huge problems and, instead, can provide a timely, inexpensive way to maintain morale, trust, and momentum throughout change implementation.

CHAPTER 6

MOMENTUM KEY 6:
Differentiate "Must" from "Nice"

When leaders differentiate what "must" be done from what would be "nice" to be done, people are able to better focus on high-priority items and let go of, or back burner, lower-priority items. Explicitly differentiating these high priorities (including expected timeframes of completion) will help everyone recognize what is critical to accomplish, especially as they are looking at all of their priorities and responsibilities. If everything seems equally important, then nothing is actually important and people make up their own priorities. This often causes people to work on the wrong priorities; therefore, they achieve the wrong goals, which ultimately lead to upsets and a loss in motivation.

Make sure messages are distinguished and prioritized in order to set the stage for momentum and success. For example, it is important to be clear that items such as overall outcome and certain deadlines cannot be negotiated. However, how something is done can be negotiable as long as, of course, it is accomplished legally and ethically. This flexibility also helps people be freed up to use their ingenuity and innovation.

Establishing clear priorities and the "right" goals has a profound impact on momentum because if people do not have a sense of achievement, they start to question why they are spending any time and energy on the change initiative. This fact explains why you don't want to be overly flexible with deadlines and deliverables — because people may begin to think the change doesn't need to be done or is not a high priority. Upward arrow 5 on the graph says, "Hold the line and finish." This is referring to the ultimate goal of the change initiative, but it could just as easily refer to all of the individual deliverables and deadlines along the way. For instance, if you have a goal of running a half marathon, you would know that sticking to a training regimen and achieving mid-term goals would be necessary to be successful. It is the same with a change initiative: holding the line on the important "must be done" items along the way is critical to reaching your final destination.

MOMENTUM KEY 7:
Tackle Change Blockers

Confront change blockers and bring about resolution quickly. The term *change blockers* refers to anyone who is resistant to the change initiative. I'm not talking about people who offer constructive criticism to help improve the change. You can identify change blockers because they are more than willing to tell you what won't work but rarely offer any ideas of substance to actually help move things forward. These people are naysayers, and they do not help to accomplish the desired goals. Change blockers also tend to act as if the three non-negotiables from Key 5 (doing what you're supposed to do, proactive honesty, and direct communication) are actually negotiable! If change blockers' voices are allowed to permeate the team, the damage can be extensive.

When change blockers are left alone, their resistance will grow and spread like a toxin throughout the team. A typical example is when people who aren't in favor of a particular change try to push the boundaries, resisting in such a way that they slow ball and stall the change. If such behavior isn't confronted, it can be a slippery slope where work is not accomplished and deadlines aren't met, halting the initiative and infecting the rest of the organization with this negativity.

For some reason, we often allow the negative people to dominate, and as you probably know, unhappy people are usually more vocal than happy people are. To exacerbate matters, we often attribute excessive power to these negative voices. Unfortunately, those voices can be so loud that we assume they represent more people than they actually do. This can cause people to react, pull back, and even make bad decisions because of the perceived negative data. For example, you have probably experienced a time when someone told you something negative and said, "Everyone feels this way." Later, you found out that only two people in a hallway had discussed it! Nevertheless, if you were under the impression that everyone on your team actually did feel something negative, you could have reacted to an inaccurate situation. To generate momentum, we need to fight this negative tendency and celebrate progress.

To help nip this in the bud, confront resistance (see upward arrow 2 on page 36) and have an upfront conversation using the three Resistance-Busting Questions from Key 4 (we also have many complimentary resources on our website www.stevengaffney.com that can aid you in this). Then, readjust your plan, including who is doing what (if needed), and keep moving forward. No one can stop you unless you allow yourself to be stopped. As my client, Scott DiGiammarino, former executive of American Express, once said, "If you can't change the people, change the people!"

Remember, time often deepens problems, especially in regard to performance and behavior. Problems rarely get better when ignored and actually tend to get worse. The higher up these issues are occurring within the organization's hierarchy, the bigger and more problematic it can be. This is because people will generally look to their supervisor for guidance about what to do — including things to ignore. This factor reveals why it is so critical to have an aligned leadership team. Leadership is about making tough decisions, not easy ones. People often put off addressing change blockers because they don't like conflict, are afraid it will create problems with the team, or they don't want to address the politics of the organization that come along with addressing the change blocker.

No Regrets: Take Action

I have worked with many people on issues related to change blockers, and not one of them has ever said to me, "I wish I had given this situation or person more time." In fact, they regret that they delayed the confrontation because once the situation was addressed and resolved through the appropriate means, the performance of the team dramatically improved. In retrospect, people realize how much could have been accomplished sooner if they had moved faster to deal with the change blocker.

The reality is that I have seen many leaders be removed because they didn't take action to solve problems quick enough; they waited too long to address and resolve the issue. If you're reading this and still debating whether you should address that one person or group of people holding you back, the mere fact that it's at the top of your mind means you need to resolve it.

Conflict can be good and helpful; leaving conflict unresolved can inhibit decision-making and become a real momentum change killer. Address momentum change blockers so you and your organization can stay focused and keep moving forward.

MOMENTUM KEY 8:
Test and Keep It Flowing

You can't fix a problem you don't know exists, and you can't use an idea that no one tells you. Therefore, open communication flow is fundamental to your change initiative and overall organization. When people are not allowed to debate, express their opinions, or share their ideas, everyone loses. Eventually, it stifles the team's motivation and momentum to move forward. Here are two critical tests to measure the openness of communication in your organization:

TEST 1— HOW OFTEN ARE THERE QUESTIONS AND DEBATE ABOUT IDEAS AND DECISIONS? If there are little of both, it is likely that at least some people are not being upfront and honest. People rarely think alike. When I am observing a team and there is little debate or few questions, then I know I am witnessing an honesty problem. Fear is often in play in these situations: fear of retribution, fear of hurting someone or damaging someone's reputation, fear of looking bad, or fear of putting someone (or themselves) on the spot. Whatever the case, it is critical to make people feel safe so they feel they can be open and share their point of view.

As we have discussed, during change initiatives, it is inevitable that adjustments will need to occur as the change moves forward and the steps are executed, and that is what makes this open dialogue so important. Open communication can help people who simply have concerns or issues feel empowered to bring them up. If they do not have an environment to voice their concerns, they could become change blockers and resist the initiative. Furthermore, we all have our blind spots — situations we cannot see clearly because we are too close to them — and during periods of change, we cannot afford to pretend those blind spots don't exist. We need others to be open and give us feedback.

TEST 2 — HOW OFTEN ARE PEOPLE SHARING IDEAS AND RECOMMENDATIONS? The voluntary sharing of ideas and recommendations is necessary for open communication and crucial to the momentum of change. The need for innovation does not end when the change initiative begins. Ongoing innovation is required because of the problems that will arise and the adjustments that will need to be made along the way. Those adjustments will demand innovative ideas. The more ideas that flow, the better your chances of coming up with the best possible solutions. When people withhold ideas, it stunts innovation and reduces momentum. To prove how often people hold back their ideas, I ask audiences, "How many of you have ideas for people but have not shared all of them?" Of course, most people raise their hands. I then follow up with, "So if the majority of you are withholding your ideas from other people, you now know that the majority of people in your life are withholding ideas from you."

The truth is that you can assume people within your organization are going to withhold their ideas — and are currently withholding them. With this awareness, you can work to create an environment where people feel free to share them. One of the best ways to encourage people to share is to demonstrate that you will actually implement at least some of their ideas. Remember that when you use people's ideas, you should let them know and give them credit. I have seen organizations reduce the flow of ideas and innovation either by neglecting to use valuable ideas or by failing to let people know their ideas were being implemented. Both cause people to wrongly conclude that it is pointless to share because it makes no difference.

Beware the Power of "No"

When we say "no," we've essentially killed an idea before it even could be considered for implementation. That's unfortunate because most ideas come to us in rough fashion; they require some modifications and adaptations. If leaders are in the habit of only accepting ideas that are well thought out or fully baked, they will find themselves rejecting most ideas and therefore sending the wrong message that they are not open to suggestions. This can kill a change initiative because the problems that arise during implementation require will require modifications, especially if problems arise. You want everyone using their ingenuity and brainpower to share in order to find the best solutions possible.

One tactical thing to do is instead of saying "no" to an idea, say "yes" and then share a condition for the "yes." For example, if an idea is shared with you but you do not see the budget to put toward it, don't squash the idea with a "no." Instead say, "Yes, I'm willing to consider the idea, and I need you to present the business case for it."

Without the free flow of opinions, concerns, and ideas, momentum cannot be maintained. As change is implemented, openness is key to provide ideas and feedback to fix the issues and keep the initiative on track.

CHAPTER 9

MOMENTUM KEY 9:
Prevent "Perfectionitis"

M ove forward with velocity. Progress should be the goal, not perfection (see upward arrow 5). "Perfectionitis" is thinking that something needs to be perfect to go out the door when less than perfect will do. Keep in mind that every day that goes by in which things are not implemented is another day that others do not get to reap the benefits of your plan. The search for perfection is the enemy of momentum.

The trouble with trying to achieve perfection and make everyone happy is that it can be exhausting. In addition, it costs a great amount of time, effort, and resources and often leads to no one being happy, let alone a great loss in momentum. In short, recognize when good enough is good enough.

With certain exceptions—like building airplanes and brain surgery—it's a rarity that something has to be perfect.

perfect. Even in those situations where the plans do need to be perfect, they don't turn out that way and, in fact, need to be recalibrated as the plan is executed. If you think about it, rarely has anybody seen a plan perfectly executed as it was designed. The truth is that the stages tend to be plan, execute, and adjust, which goes back to Key 2.

Whatever your initiative is, you're going to learn a lot as you implement and move things forward. Resist the tendency to tinker endlessly in an effort to achieve perfection. Interestingly, this is toughest for people who are high performers because they are dedicated to their work and take pride in it, so they may interpret "good enough" as mediocre.

Be aware of this dynamic and resist the demand for absolute perfection. This will require attention, because the idea that good enough is good enough does not come naturally to us. One easy way to deal with this issue is to stick to deadlines. When you start to allow deadlines to slip in order to make something better, you'll find that deadlines are constantly being adjusted; pretty soon, you'll be a year into a "three-month" project and the project still won't be launched. Bottom line is that most often, 80 percent is good enough to go out the door.

MOMENTUM KEY 10:
Don't Be Stingy–Celebrate!

One of the easiest ways to gain momentum is to communicate positive messages, achieve quick wins, and celebrate along the way. With any change initiative, it is important to break down the ultimate goal into small steps; momentum is increased when you celebrate achieving each step along the way. Unfortunately, many organizations hold back their celebration until the end goal is achieved, leaving everyone with the feeling that things are not getting accomplished. When people don't know whether goals are being met, they are prone to expect the worst and low morale sets in. People then can become resistant because they think things aren't moving forward.

To add to this, I have found that people left to their own devices focus and talk about problems rather than noticing and celebrating successes and accomplishments. This is something we must resist in our organizations. Success breeds success, so celebration is a momentum builder. Furthermore, when you have quick wins and celebrate successes, it will give the people who were initially resistant to the change a feeling that this change is different and actually working, so it will help build momentum and overcome naysayers. I am not saying to throw a party for every step of a change initiative, but at least do a good job of acknowledging the hard work and recognizing the team. People love to receive a "gold star" for their work and effort. Many times during change initiatives, good progress is being made, yet the team's morale is "doom and gloom," and their attitudes say, "Here we go again with another failed plan." This happens because no one is championing the focus and the positive news.

I was brought into a high-level change initiative where things actually were moving along and being achieved. The problem was that morale was decreasing, people were becoming stressed, and the naysayers were taking a foothold. After our analysis of the team, we discovered that the big problem was poor communication and inadequate updates to let people know that goals were actually being achieved. After executives learned how to transmit positive messages, morale picked up, momentum kicked in, the naysayers were silenced, and the change was ultimately achieved.

Focus on Accomplishments

The way you communicate to your people is a critical component of highlighting successes. For example, imagine an organization's customer satisfaction is measured on a scale from 1 to 10, and they are currently rated a 2 and need to be a 10. Many organizations would say, "We have 80 percent to go." This might create an aura of the work being an uphill battle. A better way to say it would be, "We're already 20 percent there." This is not about spinning the message — it is about focusing on the accomplishments.

One truism in life is that whatever we focus on grows. If we focus on successes, we'll get more successes. Ask any coach or player on sports teams and they will tell you that nothing cures poor morale better than winning.

Remember that input drives output. When we put positive news into the mix by celebrating accomplishments, then the output is more likely to be positive attitudes, increased morale, and the courage to take action. This will help build momentum and motivation and contribute to a successful implementation.

Bring Change to Completion

The best organizations make decisions and move forward. They are not constrained by negativity, naysayers, change blockers, or "perfectionitis." They move through their change plans with velocity, achieve goals, and reap the benefits. In doing so, they generate a positive news cycle that helps to power their change implementation. Using the 10 Momentum Keys discussed here and the accompanying Change Completion Graph will empower you and your organization to avoid the lows, beat the odds, and make changes that last.

About the Author

Steven Gaffney – Founder and CEO, Steven Gaffney Company

Steven Gaffney is the leading expert on honest communication, change, and business growth. For almost two decades, he has worked with clients on numerous change initiatives, both small and large, including mergers, acquisitions, and reorganizations.

"You can't fix a problem you don't know about, and you can't move on an idea that no one tells you. The key is to get that unsaid, said," says Gaffney.

Steven's inability to speak as a child forced him to learn the importance of effective communication at a very early age. By age three, Steven mumbled only a few words, and a doctor advised his mother that he should be placed in special classes for mentally handicapped children. Steven's mother did not accept this diagnosis, however, and doctors eventually discovered that Steven's inability to speak was caused by hearing impairments (brought on by multiple ear infections). The problem was corrected, and no one has been able to silence him since!

Steven is the respected author of five books and publications: *"Just Be Honest," "Honesty Works!" "Honesty Sells," "Guide to Increasing Communication Flow Up, Down, and Across Your Organization,"* and *"21 Rules for Delivering Difficult Messages."*

Steven Gaffney's work has been sought out by a diverse range of leaders including top military officers and chief executives of multinational organizations such as Marriott, Lockheed Martin, Raytheon, BP, SAIC, Citigroup, Allstate Insurance, Defense Logistics Agency, Northrop Grumman, Best Buy, NASA, the U.S. Navy, American Express, General Dynamics, the U.S. Marine Corps, Barrick Gold Corporation, Booz Allen Hamilton, and many others.

Steven is a cancer survivor and has brought his work into the American Society of Clinical Oncology, the Conquer Cancer Foundation, Oncology Nursing Society, and the American Cancer Society.

Steven has been interviewed and featured on major media networks and publications for the last decade. In addition, he has been a long-term regular guest on the TV show "Let's Talk Live." He also routinely makes special guest appearances on various national and local radio programs across the country.

Steven Gaffney is a Certified Speaking Professional™ and a highly respected member of the Million Dollar Speaking Group of the National Speakers Association. He is also a former adjunct faculty member of The Johns Hopkins University, as well as former board member of the Washington, D.C. chapter of Sales and Marketing Executives International. Thousands of people across the globe credit Steven Gaffney's speaking engagements, seminars, television and radio appearances, books and multimedia products with making immediate and lasting positive changes in both their organizations as well as their personal lives. This is why the leaders of the top organizations in the world say, "Get me Gaffney!"

Index